Comets

Relationships that Wander

poems by

Annie Klier Newcomer

Finishing Line Press
Georgetown, Kentucky

Comets

Relationships that Wander

Copyright © 2022 by Annie Klier Newcomer
ISBN 978-1-64662-773-8 First Edition
All rights reserved under International and Pan-American Copyright Conventions. No part of this book may be reproduced in any manner whatsoever without written permission from the publisher, except in the case of brief quotations embodied in critical articles and reviews.

ACKNOWLEDGMENTS

Previous versions of some of these poems appeared in the following journals:

The Enigmatist; Flint Hill Review; I-70 Review; di-verse-city; Interpretations #3 & #4; *Broadsheet New Zealand*; Johnson County Public Library Contest 2018, 2019 & 2022; 3elements; *Studio, New Zealand; The Coop: A Poetry Cooperative*

As a senior to have a second chance in life to develop a way to express my love of life and my love for words is something for which I give thanks. This would not be possible without the devoted editors and poets who give their time to teaching and promoting those of us who would remain silent and unnoticed without them.

Publisher: Leah Huete de Maines
Editor: Christen Kincaid
Cover Art: Abstract vector created by vectorpouch - www.freepik.com
Author Photo: Dr. Kelly Martens
Cover Design: Elizabeth Maines McCleavy

Order online: www.finishinglinepress.com
also available on amazon.com

Author inquiries and mail orders:
Finishing Line Press
PO Box 1626
Georgetown, Kentucky 40324
USA

Table of Contents

Consider Comets 1

Nepali Microcosm 3

The Broken Plate 4

The #9 5

Mother 6

Our First Bathing Suits 7

Acushla 8

Antinomy 9

Pretty Little Robots 10

T.S. Eliot's Migraine 11

Acorn Woodpeckers 12

Unsheltering In The Kansas Flint Hills 13

After The Harvest 14

The Mixed Marriage 15

Malandipity 16

A Man Walks Into An Embassy 17

The Enrollment, 1963 18

Bartering in Raglan 20

I Once Had a Mother Who Loved Me 21

Lovie Austin 22

Comets: Relationships that Wander 23

Dear World, ... 24

James Meredith 1962 picture & poem 25

For the husband who examines my written words.
For the father who taught me words are everything but nothing
if I lack a poetic life.
For the brother whose spoken words lit up every room he entered.
David, Eugene, John, you are my trifecta of inspiration.

By being seldom seen, I could not stir
But like a comet, I was wondered at …
William Shakespeare

Consider Comets

Consider which wander away and might come back.
Now wonder what has been seen for the very last time.

Some on elliptical paths that sear
the universe and disappear.

Might they come back, if I keep the faith?
Yet others defy gravity's pull, such as

when an outlier Jupiter comes too near
and poaches what is rightfully mine.

In my aphelion state I despair and
give up hope—like the Lost Children

of Israel when manna-less or as those stolen
in slave-boats from deepest Africa, never returning.

They wander off, become someone other
then who they were meant to be. Heartbreak.

I admire venturous routes that go against the norm,
brave when they flirt with the sun's ways,

never melting but still dying, creating
a separate path, though always dependent on the sun.

There is a chance they'll be forever blind
to me. Some say they are a bad omen,

foretell the death of kings. I disagree.
I say they bring a chance of something

to look forward to, with tail stretched out,
a beauty that wasn't there before and moves on.

Though I cannot deny the cry of the abandoned mother,
Come back. The anguish of the deserted wife,

Come back. The woman who looks into the mirror
and sees a face she doesn't want to claim.

We wait and we wait and we pray
in the bundled-energy that is life. We are robbed,

lied to and alone. We live watching Time pass,
for Time does not stand still in that moment of flashing across the sky,

and if distracted, takes what we cherish along with it, and even
if what matters does return, we may never again recognize.

A slow death to what we loved and once knew.
A slow death to what we thought we were planting.

Nepali Microcosm

It all depends on the order you land in
and the sherpa you end up with.

If you make the right choice,
you get to live. Guess wrong, you die.

Shuffling your feet pointed upward,
you hold on tight to your dream like a haiku

hemorrhaging words. It's hard to catch
your allotted 5 breaths per step

when you look down a 6,000 foot valley
death drop. Growing up I was fourth in the line

of a dozen young children. I side-stepped
many disappointments, like hikers on Everest

stepping over bodies who will never leave
the mountain. Often I could not see my mother

though she stood 5 feet tall at the summit
expecting us all to arrive. My dad, at base-camp,

knew better. He understood the crashing and burning.
Yes, and because he knew this, he wept watching us

squatted down on boots skiing out of control
off the mountain, he, with too few arms to catch us all.

The Broken Plate
For Chih

> *If we wonder often, the gift of knowledge will come. If we never wonder, knowledge will never find us.*
> —Arapaho Proverb

After my nephew swirled the colors,
glazed my gifts in red-rock, he smiled
and handed them to me, *Impossible to break.*

He'd dropped them before
and declared, *Unbreakable,*
his universe of plates.

Fired at Cone 10, he waited
until the kilns' duty, completed.
Love-warm, my heart absorbed the heat.

So I brought them home,
unwrapped and began placing
them into the cupboard

only to discover one fallen
star, shards too delicate
for repair.

Sadness triggered a repressed fear:
an arch crumbling
in a national park

which my grandchildren,
by the time they are born,
might never see.

The #9

Some memories breeze in and stay
like unexpected guests still in the kitchen
at 2 A.M. My new spouse disapproves,
demands I get rid of them,
then slips upstairs.

I usher the group to the front porch,
and say good-bye. As I fix a drink,
one returns, rocks back and forth
on the swing, snuggles up with the cat
who easily attaches to any lap.

I join them outside and now can't
go back in, at least not
while I remain fixated
on the #9, which always was
my deceased husband's favorite.

Mother

While getting the mail I notice
a photo of you that I pass every day.
In it you sit proper, your hair recently permed,
proud in the dress you'd carefully selected
and laid out the night before, your hazel eyes
focused on the camera, or knowing you as I do,
focused on me and paying attention for when I'd say
Cheese, ready to deliver your signature smile in time
to last forever. Is this where I mention

I miss you and can't look at your likeness
without seeing all nine of your children,
and dad mixed in hovering somewhere close by?
Most likely that day as soon as I put down
the camera, you were ready
to share a story about some neighbor
who'd moved to the block long after I'd moved
a great distance away. What was his name?
It seems important that I should remember.

I bring in the mail bundled in good news.
I dial you up as was my habit that remains
fixed even after your death. The operator says
your line has been discontinued—
like you've been unplugged. She offers to find
an alternative way to reach you
through a free directory service.
At first, a want stronger than I've ever felt
tempts me to let her try. And that's when
I remember the neighbor's name,

Vincent Nemeti.

Our First Bathing Suits

The photo my mother takes that day later shows how black and white film bleaches out the green of the background lawn fifty years ago exposing us, two small modest girls hugging ourselves until our middles disappear, innocent in our two-piece bathing suits, the first suits we remember owning. Despite the depressing heat, saturated, nearly suffocating us, we revel in our family's closeness. My sister and I dash back and forth on the lawn playing tag when my father turns on the hose, aims our way and the spray sizzles on our hot skin. We squeal. Lured in by this air of safety, we do not anticipate that by the time we choose more stylish suits, tempting teen boys, lightning will strike and the man who is our God, the one holding the hose, will be struck down.

Acushla

> *Goodbyes are only for those who love with their eyes. Because for those who love with heart and soul there is no such thing as separation.*
> —*Rumi*

Because my sister was born broken after complications
in child birth, my mother lived swimming in guilt.

In those days people looked for explanations. Not found?
Then blame was the quilt used to cover the tragedy.

While Patty's baby blanket hid her crooked and deformed body,
it couldn't protect her or my mother from the neighbors' gossip.

I didn't know I was grateful for not understanding
my mother's failed and anguished body.

Now I choose to remember my sister's soft-burnt-Irish hair
and her laugh that was her lifeline to us,

the one she used to remind us she was human,
not just the spastic movements of her flailed arms

or the legs that never could support her,
unless my father's Godly arms held her up.

The essence that was her we imagined
one day would walk on water.

Loss is when we are forced to make due
with a smattering of memories to keep us connected.

Even the ones of broken glass on the floor
from a cup that fell because her hands grew tired.

I didn't know that I was grateful
for moments when as a child I'd catch the sound

of her tender laugh before it flew up
and poof—was gone too soon.

Antinomy

Wouldn't it be wonderful if America loved
poetry? Visualize Americans cradling new words
like babies. Or words like masseuses cupping the sore
parts of our backs. I like to see poems as peace doves
I'm preparing to release over troubled seas. Sometimes
I talk with people who are more curious about
what books I read than what car I drive
because old words are full of surprises too,
like when a Latin root wraps around a French sound.
Words are golden buzzers we are anxious to push
because a poem can patch you up, mend
a broken heart or straighten a crooked thought.

My husband once bought a poetry book
at an airport kiosk. He thinks it's hidden
from me with his socks in the second drawer.
He takes the paperback out, like a mistress,
soft and sympathetic, when he thinks
I'm not looking, usually after a disagreement.
She locates the parts a wife cannot find,
delicately soothes the wounds
a spouse cannot heal, stokes his mind
the depths of which I often cannot reach.

Contemplating this fact I do his laundry. I pair his socks.

Pretty Little Robots

For the North Korean Cheerleaders at the 2018 Sochi Olympics

Fixed-eyes glimpse stars, without even tilting. They know the night sky.
Always cheering, cheering even when the stands are empty.
Dreams guarded with no shadows; though each, forever shadowed.

* Korean poetic form; even older than Haiku. *Korean "Sijo"

My T.S. Eliot Migraine

For those

    who do not understand,

April is the cruelest month,

live inside my head.

The bright lights, ebullient
stars: the lilac bushes, filtered
like poisonous gas,
pumped into a misfortunate brain,
unscheduled.

Acorn Woodpeckers

My neighbors are turning into woodpeckers,
stuffing food supplies into grocery carts like small birds
fitting acorns into pecked-out holes, creating up to 10,000

tiny storage units in a single tree. I want to place
a calming hand on their beaks, then stroke the fear
from their feathers, reassure them, It's going to be ok.

But I am all out of hand sanitizer so I start running
from sold-out store to sold-out store when I come upon
a drone attached to a leash, walking a dog. *Look,*

I yell to socially-distanced walkers on the sidewalk,
*doesn't this make you believe humans can do
just about anything?* But before I can add,

And soon we'll have a vaccine for the coronavirus,

I am on my back panting for need of air. Then I imagine
little woodpeckers on their backs too, tiny ventilators
the only thing keeping their wings afloat.

Hoarding is exhausting.

Unsheltering In The Kansas Flint Hills

My husband bought me a motorcycle today
with the idea that we can pack our things
into tidy bundles, rev up motors,
already having found someone to love,
and leave the pandemic behind.
We plan to outrace the upcoming Kansas City
hotspot of our present-day existence. Navigating
three belts of hills formed an ocean's lifetime ago,
we'll zoom off into a blazing saddles' prairie sunset.

After The Harvest in Paola, Kansas

Not barren nor dried up. Not
infertile nor The Apocalypse.
Even though the sun is too much
with us, we volunteer to pick
what's left of the sweetest of the sweet
corn. Oh orphaned food, seemingly left
to rot, ears missed by robotic fingers,
gathered by tender hands, you've been gleaned
to pass through the lips of hungry children.

Mixed Marriage

He loved the strength of Metals, Opera, Shakespeare, the Arts.
She loved pretty things, fancy dresses, a good piece of gossip,
the newspaper. They came together often enough to produce
twelve children but generally fought over things each knew well
but the other could not comprehend and wasn't about to try
to understand. Her red nail polish bled all over his pride;
his leather-bound books shut her out and somewhere between
the first and the last page, they forgot how to hold one another.

Malandipity

A teenager's lament

I killed myself the other day.
I had to die, though now
I'm not sure why.
I think it had to do
with pain, the twisted kind
which returns again and again.
As I recall, I ached
to breathe; I flinched
when touched.
All I really wanted,
was to make it stop.
I didn't think
I could make it go away
that day, or any other way.
So here I am, dead,
this much is true,
but wouldn't you know,
my pain's still here,
through all eternity,
too.

A Man Walks Into An Embassy

For journalist, Jamal Khashoggi. 1958-2018

A man walks into an embassy and he never walks out.

Like the migrating pelican seeking nourishment
found dead in Alabama, black electrical tape
wrapped around its beak, rope binding
one wing to its feet, its dark feathers
blending in with the ground cover of stone.

Like black rhinos stalked and poached for horns,
religious beliefs and fun, damaged animals
moaning, tortured before dying while bow hunters
spend hours tracking their blood trails.
Like a starfish dismembered, waiting for regeneration.

A drone of 15 lures, takes out one lone wolf. What
cowardice in this? What satisfaction in such sport?
Suitcases dripping with coral far more red
then a blood moon. The Haunting has begun. Free Speech
disappears if his words are allowed to fall off the page.

The Enrollment, 1962

For Dr. James Meredith

Some stories never end.
Discouraged, they reach up to part
the heavens, tug on the robes
of their Maker and beg to rest.
Because the storyline keeps
repeating, though, the message
needs to be re-visited.
So God says, "You are not finished.
Go back. Go back. Re-tell your story."

How can you build your mind
with no books and no pen?
What tools are left
to bring this story to an end?

When I saw this young man climbing
up steps on fire at Ole Miss
and heard the word *colored* dropped
on him by a newscaster
(as though you could color a person in-
between the lines and judge his essence),
I stopped to witness on television,
all 12 years old of me,
this memory now branded
on my brain.

How can you build your mind
with no books and no pen?
What tools are left
to bring this story to an end?

In this moment it was as if
I witnessed Moses,
resurrected, prophesying,

Let my people go.

Just like that —flanked by 30,000
troops and *Oppressed so hard*
you might have guessed that he could not
stand. # But he did not falter, relentlessly
knocking on the Ole Miss' door until
he found the Pharaoh home.

Let my people —IN.

Strong like Paul Robeson's great basso profundo voice
the young scholar's actions seen on the nightly news
still/thunder/forth from the souls of the oppressed. **

Let my people —IN.

Go back. Go back
to where the story begins,
James Meredith in the registrar's office,
Let my people in.

*Let My People Go is a phrase that originates in the Book of Exodus 5:1
** Comment feed describing Paul Robeson.
# *Go Down, Moses* is an African American spiritual published in 1872

Bartering in Raglan, New Zealand

I throw off my covers, rummage around for my waterproof
raincoat and croc sandals, unwilling to allow one in our group
to leave alone. My daughter dons her wetsuit, slippery
like seal skin, loads her surfboard onto the rental car and together
we head out of Raglan into the fog, in search of her perfect
nascent wave on Waikato Beach, famous for its black sand
and excellent surfing conditions. I'm concerned and intent to locate
her instructor who soon emerges like Neptune out of the deep mist.
Quickly they escape into the frigid ocean leaving me alone
to beach comb on deserted wet sand. The sun looms towards the horizon.

Glistening in the first rays I notice and orphaned coin.
I dig up my payment, my unexpected reward for being a good mother.
Later that day we stroll through the town, see a cart on a street corner
holding library offerings for sale. Ahh, "A Kingdom for a horse,"
or in my case my talisman exchanged for a book, with the author
pictured on the cover in a black cape soaring, like a young Shakespeare
surfing, "Sounds of New Zealand Sonnets."

Sweet Kiwi words drip from my lips
when I open to read aloud.
It's as though, for a second time that day,
treasures have washed up on my shore.

I Once Had a Mother Who Loved Me

I once had a mother who loved me before
she fell into the ocean of lost words
and speech. We journey to play on the beach
where I lose sight of her on the horizon.

Grey clouds march across the sky. We are not
certain of the monsters they push in. Finding
ourselves unprepared, we run for shelter, seems
the smart thing to do before being pummeled
by memories. We leave a drowning blue bird

on a blue wave. It is hard to look into *old*
eyes, painful to see their disturbing questions
staring back. Best to pretend we don't know
the answers. Instead we keep busy counting
our blessings, and our lists of accomplishments.

We travel alongside the Tin Man collect our heart
medal from the Wizard so we can get out
of this place. There is one, though, who stays
behind, who does the heavy lifting, who brings
mother's hand to her lips, understanding

the value of touch. When it rains it pours
heartbreaks and the caregiver is there to mend them
in ways our loving "too much" causes us "too much"
pain. So she goes back, back to find what she
sees as life but we see as dying.

I thank God for the angels among us
who understand the *long good-bye,*
who see sandcastles in the sky
where others see storms.

Lovie Austin

Yes, Lovie be a woman!
She let the good times
roll right off the tops
of her finger tips. Oh my
could those slender hands
cradle a jazz number, shake
rattle and stomp. Her music did swim,
pine, dance. Left those young'uns
swooping into a trance. Nothing could
jar them loose, except, a recluse,
The Great Depression.

*(1887–1972) Lovie Austin, a woman, was an American Chicago-based bandleader, session musician (piano), composer, singer, and arranger during the 1920s classic blues era.

Comets: Relationships that Wander

She had an arrangement with God:
She'd make the introductions.
He'd keep us safe. She placed our hands

over, then pushed our fingers on
the cold rosary beads, helping us keep track
of our prayers. She reminded us

to round up our sins each week,
even searched for them with us between
the floorboards, then dropped us off at the Church

to deposit into the Confessional. This way we could
never stray, she reasoned, we'd know our way home,
always an orderly and fail-safe orbit to her house

and to Heavenly Salvation. She hadn't counted
on comets. Didn't figure they were there
at the beginning too. Hadn't imagined her children's

choices becoming paths for maverick objects wandering
through the universe: The Stargrazers that misjudged
the distance from the eternal Bright, obliterated. Comet

Hyakutake's, 14,000 year-interval before another earth viewing,
Halley's short-term trajectory, still a 75 year wait,
and the Intergalactic that escaped entirely, never to return.

Dear World,

In conclusion:

Why do you
treat me as though
I have already left?

I am still here.

Art piece by Bruce McClain

The Enrollment 1962
(a poem to honor Dr. James Meredith)

Some stories never end.
Discouraged, they reach up to part
the heavens, tug on the robes
of their Maker and beg to rest.
Because the storyline keeps
repeating, though, the message
needs to be re-visited.
So God says, "You are not finished.
Go back. Go back. Re-tell your story."

How can you build your mind
with no books and no pen?
What tools are left
to bring this story to an end?

When I saw this young man climbing
up steps on fire at Ole Miss
and heard the word colored dropped
on him by a newscaster,
(as though you could color a person in
between the lines and judge his essence,)
I stopped to witness on tv
all 12 years old of me,
this memory now branded
on my brain.

How can you build your mind
with no books and no pen?
What tools are left
to bring this story to an end?

In this moment it was as if
I witnessed Moses,
resurrected, prophesying,
"Let my people go.

Just like that — flanked by 30,000
troops and *Oppressed* so hard
you might have guessed that he could not
stand. # But he did not falter, relentlessly
knocking on the Ole Miss' door until
he found the Pharaoh home.

Let my people — in.

Strong like Paul Robeson's great basso profundo voice
the young scholar's actions seen on the nightly news
still/thunder/forth from the souls of the oppressed. **

Let my people — in.

Go back. Go back
to where the story begins,
James Meredith in the registrar's office.
Let my people in.

* *Let My People Go is a phrase that originates in the Book of Exodus 5:1*
** *Cadence of Negro Spirituals, Paul Robeson*
\# *Lyrics in the [Moses] Moon, Let My People Go*

Anne Kirk Rosecrans 3.5.12.21

Annie Klier Newcomer was born in Cheverly, Maryland, the middle child in a family of nine children. She grew up in Syracuse, New York. Her father, a graduate professor working in metallurgy, and her older brother, a distinguish professor of Russian Jewish studies at University College London, instilled in her a life-long quest for learning and teaching. Annie graduated from the University of Illinois with a bachelor's degree in English and a master's in Education where she also had a grant to work with a Vietnamese family.

She moved to Kansas City, Missouri in 1974 and taught fifth graders at an inner-city Catholic school. In 1980 she married her husband, David, and moved to Prairie Village, Kansas where they continue to reside.

Annie became interested in writing seriously after the untimely death of her older brother in 2007. She has had short vignettes published and has had four 10 minute plays read script-in-hand by the Pot Luck Players of Kansas City, but poetry is her passion. Her poems have appeared in such eclectic places as the Grand Master Chess player and coach Susan Polgar's website, *Kansas City Voices, I-70 Review, Flint Hills Review, Coal City Review, di'-verse'-City,* Austin, Texas, Uruguay, Great Britain, New Zealand, Australia, Parks & Points poetry website and her local library's, *Poetry in the Park.*

Annie teaches poetry for Turning Point, a Center for Hope and Healing for those with chronic illnesses and is currently a poetry editor for *Flapper Press,* an online magazine. *Comets: Relationships That Wander* is her inaugural chapbook of poetry.

www.ingramcontent.com/pod-product-compliance
Lightning Source LLC
LaVergne TN
LVHW041515070426
835507LV00012B/1591